© Aladdin Books Ltd 1989

Designed and produced by
Aladdin Books Ltd
70 Old Compton Street
London W1

First published in the
United States in 1989 by
Franklin Watts
387 Park Avenue South
New York NY 10016

Printed in Belgium

Design   David West
                Children's Book De

Editorial   Steve Parker
Photo researcher Cecilia Weston-Bak
Consultant   Dr Cindy Fazey, Cei
                Urban Studies, Live
                University

*Note: The types of crimes and the
exact terms used for them vary from
place to place. A criminal act in one
country may be perfectly legal in
another. So a book like this can deal
with crimes only in general terms.*

Library of Congress Cataloging-in-Publication Data

Harris, Neil.
     Drugs and crime/by Neil Harris.
       p. cm. -- (Understanding drugs)
     Includes index
     Summary: Discusses the correlation between drugs and crime and how
the pressures experienced by drug abusers can lead to criminal acts.
     ISBN 0-531-10800-7
     1. Narcotics and crime--Juvenile literature. 2. Drug traffic-
-Juvenile literature. 3. Narcotic addicts--Juvenile literature.
[1. Drug abuse and crime.] I. Title. II. Series.
HV5801.H36 1989
384.2--dc20
                          89-31685
                                CIP
                                AC

Contents

UNDERSTANDING DRUGS

DRUGS AND CRIME

Neil Harris

FRANKLIN WATTS
New York · London · Toronto · Sydney

INTRODUCTION

Many people who start to take drugs are confident that they will stay out of trouble. They may have never broken the law before in their lives. They think that they will be able to control their use of drugs, taking whichever drug they want to, as often as they want to, and with people they choose.

But the facts show, in many cases, this does not happen. Across the world there has been a huge surge in drug use over the past 30 years, in major cities and also in small towns and rural areas. Marijuana, heroin, cocaine, crack, amphetamines, "designer drugs," LSD-type "acid" drugs and similar substances are now taken by millions of people worldwide. In many countries where these drugs have appeared, crime has increased. Drug-related crimes are numerous and varied. Some are unavoidable. Simply possessing or taking one of these drugs is illegal in most Western countries. Making such drugs, dealing (selling) them, and trafficking (transporting) them from one state or country to another, are all criminal offenses.

Crimes committed while under the influence of drugs are not as common as some people imagine. Incidents of "drug-crazed youths" mugging innocent people and looting stores were once few and far between. Alcohol, a legalized drug, is important in this respect. However, with the recent rise of crack in the United States, the pattern has changed in the past few years.

Drugs are also linked to crime by the need to buy them.

Deep in thought: is it really worth getting mixed up with drugs?

Illegal drugs are almost never free. Money changes hands (itself an offense). But the person who wishes to buy, or who has become dependent and "needs" the drug, may not have the money to pay. Users might then turn to crime. Theft, threats, prostitution and many other forms of illegal activity are mixed up with drugs.

Drug manufacture, distribution and sales are big business. They often involve organized crime. The huge profits at stake mean that the manufacturers, couriers and dealers use any methods available to make sure their business continues and there is always a line of buyers. They blackmail, extort, run protection rackets, mutilate and murder to protect their interest in this huge, illegal industry.

Some of the many links between drugs and crime are explored in this book. Drug-taking itself is a complicated issue. It is tied up with society and the conditions in which people live, their traditions, lifestyle, prospects and problems. A responsible community cannot ignore drug abuse and crime. But some experts feel that more attention to the reasons why people feel the need to take drugs in the first place, as well as the crimes associated with them, offers better hope for the future.

I never thought it could happen. One week I thought I might try drugs. The next week I was a criminal. Officially. **First-time drug offender, London.**

CROSSING OVER INTO CRIME

❝ *I sensed a creeping loneliness. I needed more drugs.* ❞

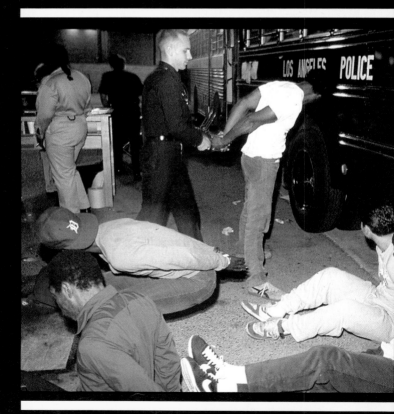

People take drugs for many reasons. Some go for the "high," the chemically-caused feeling of pleasure, or the temporary blocking out of the worries and problems of daily life. Others use drugs to be like their friends, to belong to a certain group, or to copy their "heroes." Some do it simply because it is illegal, a challenge and a kick against the rules of authority.

Drugs may be smoked, swallowed, sniffed or injected. The user may be a quiet, withdrawn person who has little contact with others, or a sociable party-goer taking the latest drug because it is the fashion. Users may be young or old, from a comfortable background or a broken home, highly-paid professionals or out of work.

Yet they all run the same risks. Once they have tried drugs, which is itself illegal, there is a greater possibility of becoming tangled up in a world built on fear and suspicion. This is the world of crime.

Forced to steal?

A teenage girl from Scotland began to take drugs occasionally. By the age of 22 she was using heroin regularly and forced to resort to stealing from her rich parents to pay for the supplies she needed. Her parents found out and, unknown to their daughter, planned to pay for a drug rehabilitation program at a private clinic. But the daughter became very upset – not so much because of her heroin addiction, but because her parents had found out that she had stolen from them. She disappeared and was never heard from again.

How much of a crime?

People rarely take drugs in order to become a criminal. Taking the drug is the significant feature, and not the fact that it is illegal. A drug user may realize that possessing and using a drug is illegal. But somehow, if it is done secretly and in private, with others of like minds, and not harming anyone else, it might not seem to them to be "so bad." Just a bit illegal, perhaps, but nothing too serious.

However, some people who commit crimes do not view the act in the same way as society in general. They often ignore the consequences, and do not even consider being caught. They do not seem to view the "law" as something that should be obeyed.

Understandably, drug users dislike being judged – just like anyone else. They may point to the fact that people are

Alcohol is a legal drug in many countries, over a certain age.

allowed to use other chemicals, such as nicotine in cigarettes, caffeine in coffee and (over a certain age) alcohol. Thousands become dependent on these kinds of drugs. So the drug user might ask: What is wrong with the occasional puff of marijuana or a snort of cocaine? Part of the answer is that society has decided these kinds of drugs are dangerous enough to be prohibited, because of their effects on the body and mind, and because of the risks of dependence.

> **❝❝The bar was full of people bombing themselves out on booze. I mentioned rolling a joint and they were horrified.** Occasional marijuana smoker who never drinks alcohol. ❞❞

From the start, the user of illegal drugs is made to feel cut off, even isolated by society at large – and especially by older generations. He or she may even be treated as downright dangerous. Some people still believe that all drug abusers are half-crazed maniacs, ready to commit terrible acts of violence.

Modern research has shown this to be untrue. Even states of severe drug dependence, as in heroin addiction, do not cause behavior like this. It is understood by doctors that a drug by itself cannot transform anyone into a criminal. The links between drugs and crime are found at a more mundane and practical level.

The commodities market
Drugs such as marijuana, cocaine and heroin are

Heroin addiction and the squalor and poverty it often brings.

commodities. But they differ from other commodities, such as food and cars. You cannot buy them on credit, or save up and buy them in a cut-price sale. There are never bargains in the drug trade – and if it seems so, there will be a catch. Organized dealers have been known to introduce drugs into areas such as housing developments at low "subsidized" prices. Yet once they have built up a list of customers, the subsidy is taken away and the prices go up. Some users have become dependent, and so they must pay the new, higher prices. In business terms, the dealers see this as an investment to increase their future trade.

Drugs are expensive, partly because they are illegal. The profit-taking barons of the drug trade do not want their commodities to be legalized. That way, they would lose control of their business and their profits would melt away. In

1986, total sales of illegal drugs in the United States were around $100 billion. This represents the "earnings" for thousands of people and their families, as well as outright profit for the few in charge.

> **❝ Drugs were my living. I couldn't get any other work. Small-time dealer.❞**

A quantity of a drug is worth as much as the dealer can get for it. There is usually someone who will pay. And the sooner the price is met, the more likely it is to rise next time. In the United States, in the late 1980s, one ounce of marijuana costs between $60 and $150. A gram of cocaine sells for between $80 and $150 and a gram of heroin for between $80 and $150. But sellers adjust the asking price according to their clients. One undercover police officer, working for the drug squad, found that prices varied by two or three times in the same neighborhood. Posing as an affluent buyer working in banking, he was asked for twice the "going price."

The need to pay for a need

Drugs might not turn people into criminals. But the need to pay for them often does. When the money runs out, crossing over into crime could seem the easy way out.

Some people have committed crimes before they use drugs. Taking drugs and becoming addicted can lead them to commit even more crime. Others turn to crime because of their need to pay for the drugs.

Regular drug use means less ability to earn, yet more to pay.

An occasional drug user may go on to develop a regular drug habit. It happens despite the user's vows that it never could. It happens without the user even realizing it. Taking more drugs costs more money. It can become a vicious cycle. More time is spent buying the drugs, being under their influence and recovering from their effects – this leaves even less time to earn the money to pay for them. Eventually, the purse is empty.

What might this mean? Some users can make sacrifices at first. In very rare cases, a user has enough money to cope, perhaps from an inheritance, but for the majority it means cutting down in some way. Cut down on record albums, going out, clothes, concerts. The drug user may start to spend more time alone or with other users. This position could in turn lead to further drug use.

> **❝❝ *I sensed a creeping loneliness. I needed more drug to feed my lonely "peace." That was the crossover point.* Former heroin user. ❞❞**

This is the stage when many people ask themselves why they should respect the law. They see society looking the other way when famous personalities are involved; but to many of these habitual drug takers, every day is a war of survival. Why should they not resort to a few "minor crimes" if their basic well-being depends on it?

Once this threshold has been crossed, there may be little to act as a brake. One of the most common crimes at this stage is small-time or "petty" theft.

Some drug users simply ignore the law. They may ignore other laws too, like speed limits on roads. Some, especially teenagers, feel "untouchable." The laws seem so far removed from their lifestyle and "good times."

The cheapest drugs?

Young people up to the age of about 16 usually do not earn money, except from part-time jobs. But that does not mean they can avoid the risks of drugs and crime. In recent years there has been an upsurge in solvent abuse, or "glue-sniffing," across a number of countries. Several solvents were involved. They were inexpensive and easily available over the counter. In a few cases, the effects were disastrous.

Sniffing glue has caused accidents, injuries and other problems.

One young boy wandered into traffic while he was "high." He was not hurt, but a driver who swerved to avoid him was badly injured.

Since the solvent products were useful household goods, they were difficult to ban. So the law was changed, making it illegal to sell them to those under a certain age. Many young people like to appear brave and daring. It became a challenge to get hold of glue and other solvents. Some succeeded. They did not really understand how they were breaking the law, or how serious the consequences might be. It seemed to them that no other ways of getting high were open. They could not afford alcohol. Yet by sniffing glue, and urging their friends to sniff, they were risking everyone's health and breaking the law.

WHY DOES IT HAPPEN?

❝ *Why did they have to catch me? Why was I the one?* **❞**

In any walk of life, it is hard to cope with an emergency. Even the most level-headed people can act foolishly in a crisis. Most of us have heard someone say: "I don't know why I did it...I suppose I was under pressure...Sorry." Or, if caught committing a crime: "I've never done anything like it before, and I'll never do it again."

People who use drugs regularly are at extra risk when a crisis occurs. Drugs create a distorted picture of everyday life. This can be a serious setback when a worried drug user, short of money, has to figure out what to do next. The chances of becoming involved in crime in such a situation are that much higher.

Everyday life already is a minefield of problems. People worry about their exams, jobs, relationships, incomes, families and friends. Some people think that turning to drugs will help to solve such problems, or at least give them a temporary break. But drug abuse can so easily bring many other problems that much closer.

❝❝ *Dozens of us took drugs. Why did they have to catch me? Why was I the one?* **Occasional user of marijuana.** ❞❞

Because using drugs is illegal, and has to be a secretive matter, users are often convinced that their offenses are minor and unimportant. They often wish the police would concentrate on "real" crime. At this stage, they do not know that they are very much part of real crime.

It is also worth remembering that very little is private these

The new drug crack is strongly linked to increasing crime.

days. To be a secret user of drugs is difficult. Family, friends and neighbors soon become suspicious. Community police and social workers are also more aware than many people realize of what is going on.

Innocent until proven guilty

Many people convicted of drug-related crimes genuinely dislike what they have done. Often they themselves cannot understand why they did it. They speak straight from the heart when they tell a court of law: "I couldn't help it, and I am truly sorry."

But every judge and police officer has heard these words dozens of times. In a court of law, they count for little. The court will want to know whether an accused person knew that his or her actions were illegal. If he or she did, and the evidence is sound, then generally the verdict will be guilty.

> ❝ *It was only when the judge said 'Guilty' and they took me to the cell that I realized what I'd done really was illegal.* **Convicted marijuana dealer.** ❞

The scale of the crime

Again and again, people charged with drug-related offenses feel shattered by the realization that they are guilty and have become criminals. Up to this point, they have taken the view that their crimes are small-time and insignificant, like driving slightly over the speed limit or "borrowing" some paper and pencils from work. The effects of the drug itself sometimes help to shield users from reality. Only when they appear in court, does the seriousness of the situation dawn on them. In the course of a few moments, they have turned from apparently respectable people into convicts with a criminal record that will follow them for many years, and in some cases, throughout life. This experience can ruin someone's self-respect forever.

Other drug users see themselves as free-thinkers, with the courage to see through what they regard as society's petty rules. They feel that being true to oneself is more important than any ideas about public duty and living within generally-accepted social rules. They may already be partly isolated from the community at large, because of their unusual views and drug-taking habits. When the trial comes to a close and the jury leader says "Guilty," bitterness deepens.

Punishment to fit the crime

The question of whether a drug user was "driven" to commit a crime, and could not stop himself or herself, usually arises only in a plea of mitigation (making the punishment less harsh, because of certain circumstances). Whether such a plea is taken into account depends to some extent on the judge and local conditions. In one court, a drug user guilty of a petty crime may be let off with a warning. On another day, in another place, it might happen that the same user would be handcuffed, led to a police van, and taken away to prison.

Some drug-linked crimes take place after careful consideration. Most of the people arrested for possessing drugs are men, and a common punishment for a minor first offense is a fine. For a second offense, it may be prison. So after a first offense, a man may persuade his female partner to take over the stealing, in order to raise money to buy drugs, and the buying of the drugs themselves. She might be "saving" him from a second offense, and jail. But now they are both thieves. Perhaps she succeeds at first. For how long? Raising the money for one "score" does not solve the problem of the next one.

Supporting the family

A single parent, especially a mother, is particularly at risk to the temptation of crime. Her children must be fed, clothed and kept warm. She may feel that only by using drugs can she cope with her situation. That adds to her sense of justification when she is hiding food under her coat in the grocery store. Prostitution (see page 33) is another way by

It is a difficult start to life for babies born to addicted mothers.

which mothers might support their children and/or their drug habit. It is certainly a desperate way to earn a living, and heartbreaking when the children eventually find out. (Prostitution is also an option for men, as well as women – mothers or not – who need to raise cash to buy drugs.)

Modern research tends to show that even women addicted to heroin are capable of being good mothers. But will such research be known to the court who hears the case? It could happen that a mother who tried to protect her children through crime, gets them taken away from her.

❝❝ *I did it for my children. But they couldn't come to jail with me.* **Mother sent to prison for drug dealing.** ❞❞

Altered personality

Many people try drugs with the idea that these chemicals will somehow improve and enrich their lives. All too often the opposite is true, and becoming involved in crime hastens the process. From being people who have lived in a basically honest way, they develop a sly cunning. In public, they have one personality, often open and friendly. But in private, they are busy forging their doctor's signature so that they can obtain drugs by prescription. Or they may be giving false information on welfare forms, or diverting money their way by feeding false information into a computer.

With a crime of forgery, there is an added strain to bear. It can take a long while for frauds to be detected. By this time, the drug user may have tried it five or ten times, even more. It is then much harder to say: "I couldn't help it."

The ordeal of prison

If someone is jailed for crimes linked to drugs, the term "petty criminal" changes its meaning. Being an "amateur" protects no one in prison. Many inmates say that the greatest ordeal of prison is the lack of privacy. And jails, like other places, have their hierarchy of the important and the less important.

❝ *We only saw him every few months, but we noticed he'd gone very quiet, lost interest in things. His parents hadn't felt it.* **Relatives of drug user convicted of credit card forgery.** ❞

The new inmate will usually have to show respect to the more experienced criminals. Refusal could mean a beating. Time spent in prison can be an unbearable ordeal. Once the prison gates clang shut, there is no use telling anyone: "I couldn't help it."

❝ *When I said I was sorry, I really meant it. I was. But they didn't take any notice. They'd heard it all before, I suppose.* Convicted cocaine-taker. ❞

DRUG-RELATED OFFENSES

" It was only a watch. He could afford a new one. "

There are many myths about drugs and crime. Two images in particular have been popular in the public's mind. One is the "addict-fiend," a drug-crazed monster who stalks innocent people in dark streets, committing horrendous crimes. The other is the spaced-out "bird-man," high on mind-bending hallucinogenic drugs, who leaps from the top of a high building with the aim of soaring into the sky, but plummets to the ground and kills himself and anyone passing by.

Both these images are fiction. Even the most extreme states produced by heroin addiction or hallucogenic drugs such as LSD rarely cause behavior like this. The truth is much less sensational. Drug-taking and crime are closely linked, but in a more mundane way. Some drug takers who are desperate for money steal, commit forgery, threaten,

The sharp eyes of the police, ever on the lookout for . . .

become dealers and sell drugs, or sell their own bodies.

Theft and burglary

Aside from the offense of drug possession, various forms of theft (larceny and robbery) and burglary are the most common crimes associated with drug abuse. Drugs users may tell themselves that petty theft is "victimless." They convince themselves that the person they stole from does not suffer. They imagine the only inconvenience is having to buy a new video recorder or watch.

❝ *It was only a watch. He could afford a new one.* **Drug user caught pickpocketing at train station.** **❞**

. . . swift and illegal exchanges of drugs and money.

The usual targets for theft are any goods that can be easily converted into cash, such as credit cards, fashionable clothes, video players, stereo equipment, cameras, radios, jewelry and valuable books. Stealing any of these items often seems to the drug-taking thief to be a once-only event. He or she refuses to see beyond the need to pay for the next week's supply of drugs. Often, the user forgets that he or she also stole last week, and the week before, and that theft – like drugs – has become a habit.

In the world of crime, most of the people who steal a video player or a camera to pay for drugs are "amateurs." They do not plan a robbery the way an experienced crook would. They do not have time to "case the joint," nor do they realize that experienced store employees and security staff can spot them straight away.

Drugs and crime are often more common in deprived urban areas.

However, shop-lifting by organized gangs is now such big business in countries like the United States, Britain and Australia, that anyone who steals can expect to be prosecuted. To the law, it does not matter if the thief has been threatened with mutilation or worse by a drug dealer waiting for payment.

A store detective described how he was alerted when two young girls came in to look at stereo equipment. He said that, in terms of the store's average customers, it was most unusual for two young girls to be thinking of buying a very expensive stereo system. However, while he and the staff were watching them, an older man made off with boxes of cassette tapes. The shoplifting gang were one jump ahead. The girls were "decoys," and they also got away in the chaos.

They questioned me and asked me to think back. I must have done dozens of jobs over the years, pinched loads of stuff. Heroin addict caught forging a credit card signature.

Generally, the more expensive the drug, the more likely the user is to resort to crime at some stage. In the British city of Liverpool a few years ago, a careful study was made of the links between drugs and petty crime. Researchers found that people who used heroin took to theft and burglary far more than those using other drugs. The main reason was that heroin was expensive.

In 1988, the chief of London's police force said that the

A drug like crack goes hand in hand with crime.

use of heroin, cocaine and other "hard" drugs in the city was increasing. He added that, in most cases, the money to pay for them would be raised through crime. This amounts to a huge amount of theft, burglary, shoplifting, drug dealing and intimidation every week, probably worth millions of dollars.

A study by the National Institute of Justice quoted the figure of $538 billion as the cost to America of crime committed by drug addicts. Drug pushers collected over $130 billion in 1987. Daily heroin users each consumed over $17,000 worth of drugs, whilst $5,000 was spent by irregular users. Daily heroin users also commit a large number of non-drug related crimes, each costing their victims $23,000 a year. In New York, the average daily heroin user distributed $26,000 worth of drugs, retaining about 40 percent in cash, or drug "wages".

Turning to dealing

Some users turn to dealing drugs with the goal of raising money to pay for their habits and also to make a profit. On paper, the idea might seem to work. For some, such a "job" offers a feeling of independence and self-sufficiency, with the added spice of excitement and even a form of "popularity." In recent years, it has been suggested that more women are being drawn to the idea of dealing, since it makes them less dependent on men.

Most dealers are in fact small-time petty criminals, or addicts who are trying to control their own supply, and dealing as a means of easing the burden of paying for the drugs they need.

Those who take to buying and selling drugs quickly find that it is a tough, dangerous business. Other local dealers,

Small-time dealing is a risky business – and illegal, of course.

already established, may resent them. Gangs try to steal their supplies, threatening them and their families with weapons. There is rarely any spirit of cooperation. Even if not found out by the authorities, the "novice dealer" may soon discover a new threat: his or her own supplier starts charging more for drugs. The laws of the criminal jungle rule. And the legal punishments for dealing are far heavier than for simple possession. Long prison sentences for dealing are common, even on a first offense.

Drawn into the web

In recent years, small illegal factories have been set up to manufacture drugs (particularly amphetamines) on a local scale. This means that the network of production, distribution and dealing lies very close to the user. The people with most to gain and lose by drug trading could live in the next street.

> **They were more like neighbors than pushers. They walked in the park, even used the library. Drug user, from a small town in the Mid-West.**

So an added risk is that, once a drug user turns to crime, he or she becomes known to these unscrupulous people. They may appear charming, and they may seem to have some sort of "credibility" because they live in the neighborhood and use local facilities. Somehow, they do not seem as dangerous as the out-of-town dealers involved in "big-time" drug distribution and bulk selling.

It could happen like this. An occasional user is approached by a contact who takes the same drug. Pleasantly, he or she asks the user to do a small favor, with comments like: "I wouldn't ask, but someone's gotten sick...I'll make it worth your while."

It seems so simple. A package has to be delivered, or certain substances must be bought from a manufacturer. No questions, no problems. The user, thinking there is little risk involved, may be glad to have the money or some drugs as a reward for this once-only "favor."

❝ ❝ *We kept our eyes open on the street. We soon knew who was getting strung out and short of cash.* Small-time dealer, Canada. ❞ ❞

Yet it is likely that the local drug trader has done some research and found that the user is short of money. One favor leads to another. If the user refuses, he or she will be threatened with blackmail. The trader will reveal that the contents of the package were illegal drugs, and the authorities might easily get to know who delivered them. The user has nowhere to turn. Like it or not, he or she has been recruited into the illegal drug trade.

Prostitution

In many places, prostitution itself or aspects of the prostitution "racket" are illegal. But men and women have turned to it to raise money in order to pay for drugs. Their problems increase. Selling sex, like selling drugs, is a vicious business. It may be run by big-time criminal organizations, for their profit. It holds many dangers, including those of sexually-transmitted diseases like the deadly condition AIDS (see page 41). In New York in the late 1980s, prostitution had become the biggest factor in the spread of AIDS among the heterosexual population.

In New York City, HIV (the "AIDS virus") was spread initially by the gay community, and then to the drug-injecting groups. Some drug injectors were also prostitutes, in order to raise money for their drugs. They passed the virus to their clients, who then passed it to other, non-prostitute partners. It is estimated that in the Bronx area of the city, two out of five males aged between 16 and 45 years are carrying the AIDS virus.

THE RISING TIDE OF CRIME

❝ *I have witnessed nothing in my life as devastating as crack.* **❞**

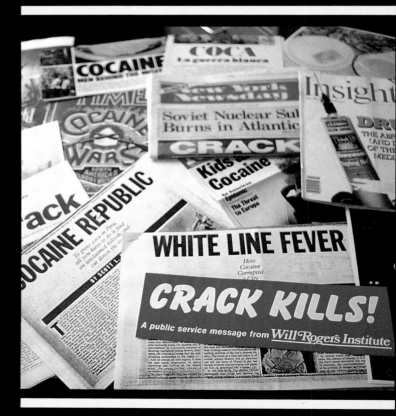

There is no doubt that drug-related crime is rising steeply in many countries. In Britain, the number of people found guilty or cautioned for drug-handling offenses rose from about 14,400 in 1979 to around 26,000 eight years later. In the United States, arrests for narcotics possession quickly approached one million per year in the mid 1980s.

Most of the British rise was due to people in possession of marijuana or small-time dealers in this drug (see page 50). However, in that period the number of offenses related to amphetamines went up more than three times, while offenses connected with heroin rose four times. There are thought to be more than 100,000 heroin users in Britain. However, in the United States in the late 1980s, heroin was thought to have become less popular compared to its high use over previous years.

There's no excuse for not knowing the harsh penalties.

The heavily fortified door of an illegal "crack den" in New York.

Issues that worry society

A survey in Scotland asked people to choose from a list of issues and say which worried them most. Over two-thirds pinpointed drug abuse, far more than were concerned about drinking alcohol, poor housing conditions or road accidents prevention.

In Los Angeles, it is estimated that more than 75,000 people belong to gangs and mobs connected with the drugs trade. Street shoot-outs sometimes occur and inter-gang killings are not unusual.

> **Small towns usually mean small drugs scenes. I don't think I could handle working in a big city all the time.** Scottish social worker.

New York City continues to provide many of the most disturbing statistics. In 1987, deaths connected with drug abuse were running at nearly three each day. These were mostly due to overdoses of cocaine, heroin, or both of these drugs, or from diseases such as hepatitis caught by using dirty needles. In 1988, there were more than five murders each day. Experts assess that a good proportion were linked to drugs, particularly crack – from fatal muggings to raise cash, to large-scale battles between gangs in the struggle to control an area's drug trade.

The crack explosion

The relatively new drug called crack, made from cocaine, has been linked with a sudden increase in crime of all types, and especially violent crime and murder.

The "gear" of narcotics use, one strand of evidence for the court.

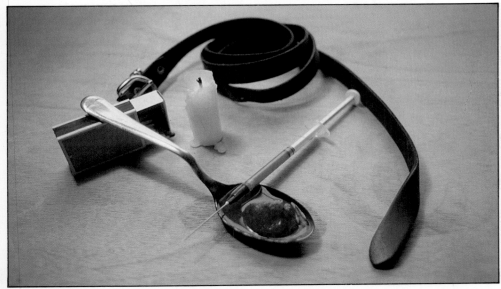

Crack first appeared in New York in about 1984. It is made by a chemical reaction created when heating ("firing") cocaine with other chemicals. The crack "rocks" so formed are smoked in a glass pipe, and as they are heated they make a cracking sound (hence the name).

Users refer to the intense, quick "high" that crack gives. After the high comes a severe "low" of depression, which the user may only be able to climb out of by taking crack again. This drug is highly addictive and extremely dangerous.

Crack has turned parts of New York, and other large cities, into "no-go" areas. "Crack dens" are rooms or apartments where crack and other drugs are bought, sold and taken. They are heavily protected with metal doors and window covers, and guarded by armed lookouts who are safeguarding their "business." Some experts, however, hold

The rising tide of popular feeling against drugs and their abuse.

the opinion that crack is not a root cause. It is yet another problem in addition to poverty, homelessness, unemployment and a high crime rate, in a society where violence is the norm.

❝ *...And their idea of fun is being in a gang called The Disciples, high on crack, totin' a machine gun.* Prince, Sign O' The Times? ❞

Crack has brought the links between drugs and crime into sharp focus, partly because it is such a powerful and addictive drug. New York City police have described how this substance underlies sudden increases in robbery, burglary, stealing cars, assaults, muggings and killings. Many crack crimes involve one dealer killing another for

The dangers of overdose are followed by the "bust" for possession.

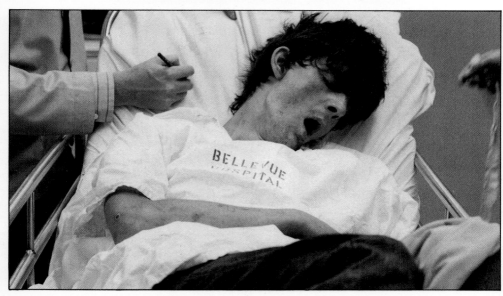

trade and money (although not while under the influence of the drug). Parents have shot their children over crack, and children have shot their parents. There are often gun battles between the police drug squads and the armed guards guarding the crack dens.

> ❝❝ *I have witnessed nothing in my life as devastating as crack.* **Former New York City cop, now a state worker in drug abuse services.** ❞❞

AIDS and the illegal market in needles

One of the most common ways to catch the virus that causes AIDS is to use a "dirty" needle or syringe for drug injection. This means a needle or syringe already used by someone else, which could be infected by the virus, and which has not been sterilized properly after use.

Campaigns to warn drug injectors about AIDS and the dangers of dirty needles have met with a degree of success. But instead of stopping drug use, in the United States some injectors have become involved in a black market. "Clean" syringes and needles are stolen from pharmacies or warehouses, by the users themselves or by others, to sell at a profit. In some areas the black market is highly organized, with corrupt physicians signing over large supplies of needles and syringes.

In 1988, Britain's Advisory Council on the Misuse of Drugs put forward the view that the dangers of AIDS and its associated risks could be greater than the problem of drug abuse. It suggested that drug injectors should be provided with free sterile needles, to slow down the spread of AIDS. In the late 1980s, experimental projects were set up in New York to supply participants with free, clean needles, in order to study the effect of this process.

Another recent rise in crime is linked to the epidemic of AIDS. This condition is fatal, although it can take many years from catching the virus that causes it, to developing the disease itself.

BIG-TIME DRUG CRIME

" *You feel helpless, you can't get back at them.* "

The illegal traffic in drugs exists to make profit for its manufacturers and dealers. Users might talk about "highs" or "psychedelic" experiences while under a drug's influence. But users do not run the illegal drug industry. The people who control the business are generally tough, ruthless operators who are only interested in the huge profits it generates.

There is a long chain of distribution in the drug industry. It begins with the so-called drug barons who grow coca (for cocaine and crack) in South America, or cultivate poppies (for heroin) in Asia. By the time a supply of drugs reaches the country where it will be sold, it has already secretly passed through many hands. At every stage, people commit crimes and take huge risks – and are illegally paid large rewards. There are landowners, harvesters, negotiators, couriers and

The start of the drugs trail: opium poppies in a quiet valley.

smugglers, operators of planes and boats and trucks, corrupt security guards and crooked customs officials. It is a long chain of criminal activity.

> ❝ *The screwed-up kids here, in my town, are keeping the drug barons in luxury.* **Drugs officer from Birmingham, England.** ❞

Less drug, more profit

The drug itself changes as it passes along the chain. With each sale along the line, dealers multiply their profits by adding other substances (like lactose or sugar) to the drug to "bulk it out." The weight (and so the value) of the packet goes up, but its purity goes down. A professional trafficker usually knows how to test the quality of a drug batch. But by the time

The war against drugs is being fought the world over.

the batch reaches the local distribution area, no one will really know what it contains. That, however, will not stop each dealer in turn from reducing the purity still further in order to increase profits.

What started out as a kilogram of almost pure heroin may be less than one-third heroin (the rest being sugar or even chalk) by the time it reaches a local distributor. In the twilight world of drugs, there are no controls over the way the drug is diluted. One batch of "heroin" was seized by police and it was found to be mixed with the poison strychnine.

> ❝ **You never know what you're buying. But good smack or bad, you go for it cause you need it. Heroin addict.** ❞

Eventually, the drug consignment reaches its main selling zone. This might be a whole town, or part of a large city like New York, London or Sydney. Its arrival will have been advertised as part of the "business marketing technique." On the drug grapevine there will be rumors about the arrival of a batch of crack, or Lebanese hashish, or amphetamines. This gives people time to raise money for payment. It also helps to generate a line of customers as the word gets around and expectations grow.

The power game
If the drug is cocaine or heroin, the local "wholesaler" probably sells at around 45 percent purity. By the time it reaches the street dealers this purity is down to about 35

percent, and at times of supply shortage it may be as low as 10 percent. So far in the process, every buyer has made a profit. Money means power, and each buyer has some power over somebody else. A dealer with a batch of cocaine or acid to sell can play clients off against one another.

But when the ordinary user buys from the street dealer, the chain of power comes to an end. The user has no one to sell to, and so has no influence. He or she pays the asking price, and may end up injecting 10 percent drug and 90 percent chalk or even brickdust. Users are the most vulnerable and exposed people in a long enterprise that began thousands of miles away. This is exactly what the big-time growers, smugglers and dealers want.

> ❝ *If the dealer didn't show, it wasn't the end of the world. I wasn't hooked. But you feel helpless, you can't get back at them.* **Regular user of cocaine.** ❞

Fighting drug crime

The war against drugs is one of the most concerted international efforts in history. Almost every police force in the world has large teams of drugs specialists. Many, such as the United States, also have federal forces and government agencies set up to fight the narcotics trade. There is also Interpol, the worldwide police intelligence organization, and a variety of smaller, but expert units to combat the drug trade and catch smugglers and traffickers in the air and on the high seas.

Fleets of surveillance ships patrol the waters around regions such as Britain, mainland Europe and Australia, as well as stretches of the United States, like the Florida coast. Customs staff watch ports and airports, gathering information and acting on tip-offs. They search suspicious cargo, and if drugs are discovered, they may let the trafficking continue in order to catch each stage of the criminal chain. Extradition treaties are signed so that suspects can be sent from one country to another, to be put on trial. Billions of dollars are spent every year in chasing the traffickers.

A vast and illegal network lies behind each local drug dealer. If, for any reason, a local dealer is threatened, he or she is more likely to reveal the names of users rather than identify the bigger suppliers. In many cases the local dealer's supplies come through such a complex route that the background suppliers cannot be traced.

As governments intensify the pressure on drug dealers, so the climate of fear increases. Like the cost of the drug, this fear has to be spread down the chain of distribution. But whether the ordinary user wants to or not, he or she has no one to threaten. The drug users on the streets of Paris, Glasgow or Chicago should not think the influence of the drug barons is limited to their own poppy fields or coca plantations. The violence and menace which they generate is felt all the way down the line.

The race for new products

The people who run the illegal drug industry can be very inventive. Like all businesses, they like to come up with new products and so increase profit. "Here, try these," says someone at a party, handing out multi-coloured tablets. There may be no charge, at first. But the drug's effects are being carefully noted by someone. This is the market research of the drug business. Somewhere, a long way away from the party, a tiny illegal factory is making these new pills by the thousand. When people like them enough, they will start to pay for them. Then the price will rise. Crack in particular, as explained earlier, has been a "dream success" for the illegal drug business.

Protecting their interests

In dozens of countries, including in North America, Europe and Australia, dealing in drugs on a large scale can bring life imprisonment. In some states, such as Malaysia, the death

Warning: drug-dealing means the death penalty in some countries.

penalty has been introduced for this offense – and it has been carried out. People who buy and sell drugs are literally risking all, including their wealth, their liberty and their very lives. So it is likely they will be totally ruthless in protecting themselves.

The big-time drug dealers, the "Mr. Big's," are business people. Drugs are their commodity. Like any business operators, they wish to protect their earnings. This means that the drugs they make and sell must never be legalized, or the "industry" would become full of traders, and profits would fall. It also means that, almost every day, the big dealers arrange bribes, threats and murders for anyone who stands in their way.

In their own countries, such as Burma, Thailand, Pakistan, Colombia, Nepal, Peru, Lebanon or Bolivia, the big-time drug barons are often prosperous and influential people. (Peru is said to earn $400 million each year from drug profits coming back into the country and being spent there.) Governments may listen to what they say. They live in style and wealth and have high ambitions for their children. Very often, they send their sons and daughters to well-known colleges in Europe or North America. But they would become angry parents if these sons and daughters began to use marijuana or cocaine. They know the risks involved.

Changing times

As recently as the 1970s, the marijuana market in Britain was the realm of amateurs. Many dealers in this drug were small-timers, and they were convinced it was not as harmful as nicotine or alcohol. They led a crusade to try and inform the public of their views. They campaigned for marijuana to be made legal, and they took little or no profit from its distribution.

But times have changed. The British marijuana scene is now the realm of organized criminal gangs. They have no interest in the debate about whether this drug is hazardous or not. Their organization was in place long before they turned to marijuana as a way of making illegal profits. To them, it is just another addition to their illegal business empire, just another way of making money.

Free-wheelers

There are many other operators involved in illegal drug trafficking. Between the highly-organized gangs at one end,

Cannabis for marijuana – source of wealth for the criminal few.

and the occasional user-dealer at the other, are those people known as "free-wheelers."

A typical example of a free-wheeler is the business person escaping from political events. At the time of the Iranian revolution in 1979, some wealthy families decided to move out of the country. They may have been blameless people up to that point. Perhaps they had much to fear from a new regime. But in some cases their wealth lay in immoveable items such as factory equipment or farming land. This could not be taken out of the country. One "answer" was to turn to crime – sell out and invest in the highly-profitable, but illegal, drug trade.

In many developing countries, political change occurs very quickly. It does not always happen in an orderly way, governed by the rule of law. This means that from all corners of the world, there will be desperate people whose survival has taken them into large-scale trafficking.

Drugs for guns

There is one more aspect of the drug business to consider. An occasional drug user in Los Angeles or Liverpool may feel little in common with an armed struggle in a faraway land. But when drugs are paid for, the money may work its way back to put a gun in someone's hands. Drug money has persistently found its way to terrorists and other armed groups. In 1989 an armed struggle developed in Colombia, as the government clamped down on drugs, while the criminals bombed, murdered and created havoc in attempts to protect their interests.

COPING WITH THE PROBLEM

" *At the time, I felt everyone was against me.*

One way or another, any drug can be destructive if taken to excess. Some drugs do this chemically, by their effects on the brain and body. Others, through user's need for money to buy them, especially for those who become dependent. Some do it by the company and lifestyle they encourage. Often, these factors combine. The user gradually loses his or her grip on life, and progresses from the single crime of possessing an illegal drug to the multiple crimes of theft, extortion, dealing and other offenses.

A move to improve?

Attitudes toward drug abuse are slowly changing. In some countries, like the United States and Britain, some doctors or clinics prescribe substitute drugs to addicts. For

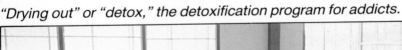

"Drying out" or "detox," the detoxification program for addicts.

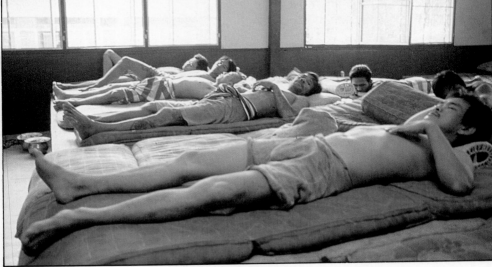

example, users who are dependent on heroin may be prescribed methadone. This may help in several ways. One is that the addict has a regular, secure source of the drug. This is important because it acts as a basis from which he or she can try to break out of the vicious cycle of crime – raising money to pay for the habit. Also, the addict may be able to slowly stop taking the drug, in a controlled way, and eventually become "unhooked."

However, such schemes are rare compared to the total number of drug takers. Nevertheless, in Britain, the policy of preventing the spread of HIV infection has meant that more and more doctors are providing injected drugs on controlled prescriptions.

Prevention is better

Drug users may feel that society has a grudge against them. They may say that they take drugs only occasionally, and harm no one – perhaps not even themselves. So why should they be punished? Certainly, many users feel they are unfairly victimized. Some believe that they are being hunted and persecuted. Others claim that their motives are being attacked. They believe no one has sympathy for their reasons in using drugs, and that if society was fairer and more just, then perhaps they would not be tempted into drug use. Some are even left feeling that their very thoughts have been made illegal.

But, most of the time, it is not the drug user as an individual who is being sought. More and more, what worries the people in authority is the drugs themselves, the habits and

Another success as a secret drug factory is raided and destroyed.

lifestyles they bring, the damage that a pregnant woman can do to her unborn child through drugs, and the need to contain the illegal drug trade at all levels. No one is trying to stop people from relaxing or freeing themselves from worry. There are many ways of doing this, from meditation through sports and games to concerts and dancing. What society is trying to do is prevent a mistake that could ruin a life.

Labeled for life

One problem with the combination of drugs and crime is that, very often, it can never be put right again. A user who is caught and branded a thief or crook will have to live with a criminal record for years. It can affect school, job and relationships. If a user gets into hopeless debt, then even after he or she reforms, it may take years to pay off.

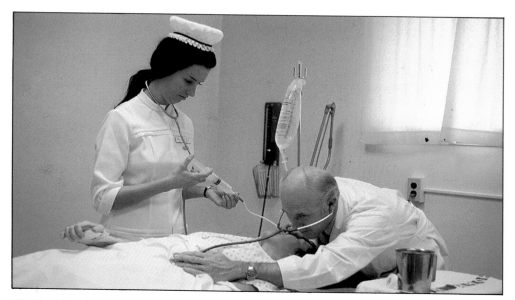

Paying for drugs with the ultimate price – a human life.

 I got caught by the police early. That was about 12 years ago. At the time, I felt everyone was against me. Now I see, they were really for me. Drug user arrested at 18 years of age.

There is one way to steer clear of all these risks and dangers. Don't get involved with drugs. Remember that, if you start taking drugs, you will never really know where they will lead you – you only think you know.

FACTFILE

The drug laws

The laws governing drugs are wide-ranging (see opposite) and the police have great powers to stop, search, remove property and ask people in for questioning.

In the United States, Articles 220 and 221 of the Penal Law deal with the penalties attached to the unlawful trade in mind-affecting drugs. These articles are compatible with the Public Health Law. They set the criminal penalties for possession or sale of drugs considered to be harmful, or subject to abuse. Such drugs include heroin, crack and cocaine.

The penalty can vary from a misdemeanor (which can mean up to 3 months in jail, or a $500 fine), to an A-1 Felony, which comes a minimum term of 15 to 20 years and a maximum life term. The seriousness of the penal depends upon the individual drug, and the amount held and sold.

The cost of crime

The cost of the drug-linked crimes committed by drug users is only part of the overall cost to society.

For example, there are the costs of the person-hours for police officers investigating incidents. There is upset, worry and time off work for the victims of burglaries and thefts. There is a strain on the hospital and health services for drug overdose victims, and those injured during fights and muggings connected with the drug trade.

There are direct costs for authorities involved in the fight against drug-related crime.

There are court costs, lawyers' fees, remand expenses, and finally the price of prison itself.

Balanced against this are the fines paid by drug offenders, which are tiny in relation to the costs. Recent powers have allowed the courts to seize money, property and other assets from convicted drug manufacturers and dealers.

Illegal drugs seized in raids are destroyed.

DRUG PROFILES

Heroin

A powerful opiate drug made from the painkilling drug morphine, itself made from the opium poppy. It can lead to addiction.

In the United States, heroin and related opiates are regulated under the Controlled Substances Act, and come into class 1 of the act. This means it is against the law to possess or supply them without a prescription or special license, or to make, export or import them without the proper authority. It is also illegal to allow premises to be used for making or supplying such drugs.

Cocaine and crack

Cocaine is a powerful stimulant drug made from the leaves of the coca shrub. Crack is made from cocaine by a chemical reaction.

Cocaine and related substances are regulated under the Controlled Substances Act, in class 1, as for heroin.

Amphetamines

These are stimulant drugs, formerly used against depression and as "slimming aids". Today they are prescribed by doctors only in special circumstances.

Amphetamines are legal if prescribed correctly by a doctor and in the possession of the person for whom they have been prescribed. Otherwise, amphetamine itself and the related drugs phenmetrazine and methylphenidate are regulated under the Controlled Substances Act, in class 2. If they are in injectable form, they may be in class 1.

Marijuana (cannabis)

A relaxant drug, usually smoked, and made from the leaves or other parts of the cannabis plant. "Hashish" is the resin or "sap" scraped from the plant.

Cannabis is regulated under class 2 of the Controlled Substance Act. Except under special license, it is against the law to possess, supply or sell the drug, or to grow or prepare the plant and its parts. It is also illegal to allow premises to be used for growing, supplying or taking it.

LSD ("acid") and hallucinogens

LSD is a synthetic chemical used to give hallucinations on a "trip." Many similar drugs have been developed in recent years. These drugs are strictly regulated under class 1 of the Controlled Substances Act, as for heroin.

SOURCES OF HELP

Various organizations will give confidential advice about drug-related problems, including the legal problems involved with simple possession of a drug. However, for those people who begin to get involved in dealing, stealing and other more serious drug-linked crimes, the situation rapidly becomes more complicated. There are no easy answers.

National hotlines

National Cocaine Hotline
1 (800) C-O-C-A-I-N-E

This is a national toll-free number that provides callers with counseling twenty-four hours a day.

National Institute on Drug Abuse
Treatment Referral
1 (800) 622-H-E-L-P

This hotline is staffed from 9:00am to 3:00am on weekdays and from 12 noon to 3:00am on weekends. Counselors can talk with you, refer you to a drug treatment program, or answere questions about drugs, treatment, health or legal problems.

New York State Division of Substance Abuse
1 (800) 522 5353

This toll-free number reaches counselors who can provide referrals for treatment or legal advice, or over-the-telephone crisis intervention.

National Federation of Parents for Drug Free Youth
1 (800) 554-K-I-D-S

This is not a crisis hotline, but a place to call for drug information. This educational organization provides both parents and kids with informational pamphlets, books, and videos.

Self-Help Organizations

Cocaine Anonymous
263A W 19th Street
New York, NY 10011
(212) 496 4266

This is a self-help group modeled on Alcoholics Anonymous. To find a local chapter near you, call the number above.

National Self Help Clearinghouse
33 W 42nd Street
New York, Ny 10036
(212) 840 1259

Can provide information on self-help rehabilitation organizations in your area, or put you in touch with one of the twenty-seven state and local self-help clearinghouses around the country.

Drug Treatment and Rehabilitation Programs

There are 8,000 to 10,000 drug treatment programs across the country. These include inpatient (residential) and outpatients facilites, covering a range of services: detoxification, counseling, family intervention, aftercare.

National Association on Drug Abuse
355 Lexington Avenue
New York, NY 10017
(212) 986 1170

Conducts a drug prevention program and offers family counseling.

Helping Youth Decide
National Association of State Boards of Education
PO Box 1176
Alexandria, Va 22313
(703) 684 4000

Write for their free booklet about making informed decisions concerning drugs, alcohol, smoking and other issues. This organization also organizes parent-student workshops and community projects.

Legal Advice

Department of Justice
Drug Enforcement Administration,
Washington D.C. Division
400 6th Street S.W.
Washington,
D.C. 20024

WHAT THE WORDS MEAN

Note: the exact meanings in law of terms such as burglary, larceny, robbery, theft, etc. vary from region to region. The following are general descriptions only, and not the full legal definitions. Consult a lawyer or solicitor for further information.

burglary breaking into or entering another person's premises with the intent to steal or commit a similar crime. In some places, burglary is still defined as occurring at night. In other places, there is no distinction and burglary may occur at night or in the daytime

courier in the illegal drug world, a person who conveys a consignment of drugs from one state or country to another, breaking the law in doing so, and thereby running the risk of fines and imprisonment, or even death, if caught

crack a drug similar to cocaine and prepared from it, but with faster and more intense effects, and known to be highly addictive

dealer a person who sells drugs, either internationally, or at a local level such as in a small town or in one neighborhood of a city

drug any chemical or other substance that changes the body's working (including the way the person's mind works, his or her behavior, etc.)

drug abuse non-medical drug use with harmful effects, on the abuser and possibly on others

drug baron an everyday term for a person in charge of a large drug manufacturing and/or distribution organization, who is usually exceedingly rich due to the illegal but high profits of this business

drug misuse using drugs in a way which people in general would see as not sensible, or not acceptable, and possibly harmful

larceny "theft" in which a person takes away someone else's property (from a handbag to a bank note, a stereo system or legal documents), with the intent of keeping it, and without that person's permission. Compare *robbery*

petty crime law-breaking incidents, such as snatching a wallet or shoplifting a sweatshirt, which may seem small-scale and minor in the general scale of crime, when compared to, for example, murder. However, every crime affects someone

robbery larceny with force; "theft" involving violence or intimidation

shoplifting taking goods from a shop or store without paying for them, and with the intent not to pay for them

suspended sentence a prison term which is not served at the time, but which will take effect if the person commits another crime

theft a general term for taking something that does not belong to you, with the intention of keeping it, for example, as in larceny and robbery

trafficker a person who deals in drugs, distributing and selling them

INDEX

The publishers wish to point out that all photos appearing in this book were either lent by an agency or shot with posed models.

Photographic Credits:
Cover and pages 4, 11, 17, 19, 22, 27, 30, 35, 36, 37, 40, 41, 43, 45, 49, 53, 54 and 59: David Browne; page 7: Frank Spooner Agency; pages 9, 13, 38: Magnum Photos; page 15: Roger Vlitos; page 28: Mike Goldwater/Network; pages 31 and 56: Associated Press; pages 44 and 57: J. Allan Cash Photo Library.